NATIONAL GEOGRAPHIC

BAY
IN THE BALANCE

PATHFINDER EDITION

By Emily Murphy and Greta Gilbert

CONTENTS

SAVING THE BAY'S BOUNTY

IMAGINE A BODY OF WATER so full of life, you could simply reach down into it and grab your dinner. For thousands of years, that's just what people living near Chesapeake Bay could do. The Chesapeake Bay's vast, shallow waters nurtured a bounty of seafood, including fish, crabs, oysters, and clams. Today, however, that bounty is at risk. Read on to find out why.

A New Day? *Scientists and leaders are working hard to make Chesapeake Bay's health as golden as this sunrise.*

I T'S MORNING ON CHESAPEAKE BAY. From high above, the bay appears still and calm. But from its shores, it is bustling with activity. Men and women are getting ready for a day on the bay. Ropes are tied. Crab pots are secured. Fishing lines are checked. Boat engines rev. At last, all is finally ready.

Scores of boats stream into the bay. Their captains are harvesting the "fruit of the bay." Some are looking for the bay's famous blue crabs. Others are fishing for rockfish. Some are searching for oysters and clams. Each year, fishermen and women take 500 million pounds of seafood from the bay. Their catch includes one-quarter of all oysters and one-half of all clams and crabs eaten in the United States.

Fishing from the bay is not new. It has provided food for centuries. That may end soon. You see, the Chesapeake Bay is in trouble.

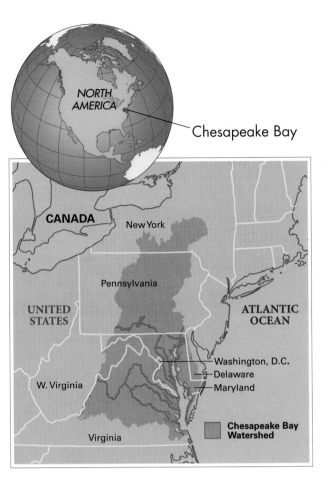

NORTH AMERICA

Chesapeake Bay

CANADA

New York

Pennsylvania

UNITED STATES

ATLANTIC OCEAN

W. Virginia

Washington, D.C.
Delaware
Maryland

Virginia

Chesapeake Bay Watershed

A Mixing Bowl

To see what is happening to the bay, we first have to learn what it is. The bay is an **estuary**. An estuary is a wide area of water that marks the place where a river meets the ocean. Salt water from the ocean and fresh river water mix together in an estuary.

The Chesapeake is the largest of 130 estuaries in the United States. It is 200 miles long and has over 11,000 miles of winding shoreline. More than 150 rivers flow into the Chesapeake. The bay holds 18 trillion gallons of water.

The bay is so large that its **watershed** touches six states and Washington, D.C. A watershed is an area that surrounds a body of water. All the water in the Chesapeake Bay watershed flows into the bay.

Many different kinds of plants and animals live in or near the bay. About 3,600 species depend on the bay for survival. Without the bay's special blend of fresh and salt water, many of those species would die out.

Why Is the Chesapeake Bay Important?

Many kinds of plants and animals live in or near the bay.

The bay provides many jobs.

The bay helps to control floods.

People enjoy the bay.

Troubled Waters

Plants and animals share the bay with people—lots of people. Nearly 16 million people live nearby. Everything they do affects the bay and the rivers that flow into it. For example, rainwater washes pollutants from driveways, farms, lawns, parking lots, and roads into the bay. Even air pollution affects the bay. Pollutants from cars fall back into the bay directly, or together with rain and snow.

Some pollutants cause too much **algae** to grow in the bay. Algae are plants. They feast on many pollutants. Sometimes algae cover large areas of the bay. The algae block sunlight. That's bad news for plants such as grasses, which need sunlight to grow. As the algae covers the surface of the water, it also uses up oxygen in the water. Without enough oxygen, plants and animals die.

Blue crab

The Bay Begins Here. *Dirty water from this Maryland parking lot will reach the bay.*

Day on the Bay. *A heron and two people share the shore of Chesapeake Bay.*

Trash Trouble. *Trash pollutes the water of Baltimore Harbor in Maryland.*

Chesapeake Bay Report Card

	Categories	Grade	Score	Score Change
POLLUTION	Nitrogen	F	16	-1
	Phosphorus	D-	23	none
	Water Clarity	F	16	+2
	Dissolved Oxygen	D	19	+5
	Toxics	B+	28	+1
HABITAT	Forested Buffers	C+	58	+2
	Wetlands	D-	42	none
	Underwater Grasses	D+	22	+2
	Resource Lands	A	31	+1
FISHERIES	RockFish	B+	69	-1
	Crabs	F	50	+15
	Oysters	F	5	+1
	Shad		9	none

Source: Scorecard—State of the Bay in 2010, *State of the Bay Report 2010*, Chesapeake Bay Foundation, p. 3.

Tracking Progress

Things are getting better, though. Many people are cleaning up the bay. In fact, the bay is cleaner now than it was in 2008. How do we know? Report cards!

Every year, organizations working to protect the bay issue reports cards. Like many school report cards, Chesapeake Bay report cards give number and letter grades in different categories.

In 2010, for example, one organization gave the bay low grades in its "pollution" categories because too many pollutants were washing into the rivers that flow into the bay. However, the bay got a high grade in the "crabs" category because the population of blue crabs throughout the bay had improved.

It may sound simple, but using grades to score the bay's health is a big deal. Report cards help people understand the bay's problems and celebrate improvements. In fact, it has been so effective that the approach is now used in restoration projects across the United States.

Tracking progress is a good thing. After all, the bay's health affects everyone. It affects the water people drink and the fish they eat. A healthy bay means healthy people.

WORDWISE

algae: kind of plant

estuary: large body of water where fresh and salt water mix

watershed: area whose rivers all flow toward the same point

Critical

Thousands of animals depend on the Chesapeake Bay for survival. All are important, but some, called keystone species, are absolutely essential to the bay's health. Others, called indicator species, are extremely sensitive to changes in the bay. Tracking the number of keystone and indicator animals is another way to measure the bay's health. Meet some of these critical critters.

Are blue crabs really blue? Their claws are! As both predator and prey, blue crabs play a keystone role in the bay's food web. These bottom-dwelling swimmers will eat anything they can find, including oysters, snails, grass, and fish. The crabs, in turn, feed fish and birds, and even other blue crabs! They are also important to thousands of fishermen and women. In the past, overfishing and habitat loss caused blue crab numbers to decline. Today, tighter limits on crabbing have helped improve their numbers.

Two hundred years ago, thousands of river otters wrestled, rolled, and dived along the shores of the Chesapeake. Over time, however, trapping, loss of habitat, and pollution dramatically reduced the population of this important indicator species, and eventually otters disappeared from the area. When they were reintroduced to the Chesapeake region in 1982, people weren't sure they would survive. To everyone's surprise, they did! Scientists find it difficult to count these notoriously shy animals, but believe their populations may be growing in some parts of the bay—hooray!

Critters

By Greta Gilbert

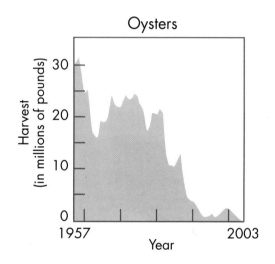

1 gallon + 0.3 gallon

An oyster can filter 1.3 gallons (5 L) of sea water per hour

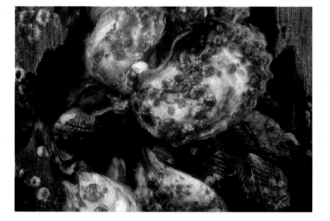

Oysters

Harvest (in millions of pounds)

30

20

10

0

1957 — 2003

Year

Eastern oysters may not be pretty, but no other species filters, or cleans, water more beautifully. By sucking algae and other food particles from the water, a single oyster can filter as much as 1.3 gallons (5 L) of water per hour. Oysters were once so plentiful that they were able to filter the bay's 18 trillion gallons of water in less than a week. Disease, pollution, and overharvesting have caused oyster populations to decline. Today, their numbers are only 1 percent of what they were in the 1950s. The importance of their filtering ability to the bay plus their sensitivity to pollution make oysters both a keystone and an indicator species.

BRINGING UP
Baby

Oyster Nursery. *Jamie (left) and Casey display a completed Taylor Float. It will house about 2,000 baby oysters.*

Oysters

By Emily Murphy

SCHOOL IS OUT for the day, but work has just begun for Casey Lowe and Jamie Johnson. The two middle schoolers live in Arnold, Maryland, near the Chesapeake Bay. They belong to a local Student BaySavers group. Today the students are making homes for thousands of baby oysters called spat.

"We are trying to increase the oyster population, which has almost vanished," Casey explains. Some oysters died from diseases or pollution in the bay. Others disappeared because people caught so many that the oysters couldn't repopulate quickly enough.

Oysters are important to the bay because they act like pollution filters. Like filters in a fish tank, oysters suck in impure water around them and pass out clean water. An adult oyster can filter, or clean, almost 60 gallons of water a day.

The oyster homes that the BaySavers are making are called Taylor Floats. They are about the size of a bathtub and are made out of plastic pipes and netting. The floats rest on the surface of the water where plants called algae grow. The baby oysters, which come from a University of Maryland lab, will spend the next five months in floats. They will eat algae and grow quickly.

Each BaySaver will look after a float. Jamie is going to tie her float to the dock in the waterway in her backyard. She and the other BaySavers will make sure the baby oysters have enough to eat and do not get covered with dirt.

"When the oysters are grown, we will release them into an area in the bay where fishing is not allowed," Jamie says.

"The bay is a very special place," Casey notes.

Jamie adds, "We have to help because we live here, too."

Assembly Line. *Workers glue plastic pipes together to make a frame. Netting comes next.*

Moving Day. *BaySavers lower baby oysters into their new home. The oysters will spend the winter floating next to this dock.*

Save the Bay

Now it's your turn! Answer these questions to save the bay!

1 What is an estuary? What kinds of water mix there?

2 How does human activity affect the Chesapeake Bay?

3 How do the people working to clean up the bay keep track of their progress?

4 Why do scientists pay special attention to the number of animals such as otters in the bay?

5 How do groups like BaySavers help keep the bay healthy?